Prayers for Real Women

OVER 150 PRAYERS OF BREAKTHROUGH FOR WOMEN

NATALIE BRECKENRIDGE
MINISTRIES

Dedication

To my beloved Belle,

Your beautiful and precious life has taught me constant and consistent prayer. I remember you always when I pray. I love you baby girl. You light up my entire world. There is nothing more beautiful than your precious smile and silly giggle. Nothing makes me more proud than worshipping beside you.

XOXO,
Mom

Table of Contents

High	Narcissistic
Home	Negative
Hothead	Nosy
Husband	Numb
Immature	Obedient
Impatient	Obsessed
Innocent	Offended
Inspire	Oil
Israel	Opinions
Indirect	Organize
Jaded	Over It
Jealous	Panic
Joy	Passion
Kind	Passive aggressive
Kiss	Petty
Karma	Powerful
Kitchen	Poverty
Know It All	Prepare
Late	Pure
Light	Purpose
Love	Quiet
Logic	Quenched
Loyal	Quit
Lonely	
Mad	Radical
Manipulate	Realistic
Maternal	Religion
Marriage	Real
Messy	Relax
Money	Rest
Moving	Resent
Moody	Salvation
No	Secret
Nag	Selfish

Sex
Skeptical
Shy
Spirit
Success
Tears
Testimony
Tithe
Tolerant
Tradition
Ugly
Uncertain

Useless
Virgin
Vague
Vulgar
Vulnerable
Weak
Worth
Worry
Why
Yell
Yourself
Zeal

Introduction

Girl, you better pray. Inside the pages of this book are much more than mere words and nice thoughts. There are prayers that can and will change your life, if you let them. The Word of God is alive and active, sharper than any two edged sword and when used as a weapon; it can defeat any enemy.

My prayer isn't that you would run to these pages every time you need to speak with The Lord, but rather it is my deepest desire that these prayers would help you learn to pray. Prayer is a muscle and it is built through the trials and celebrations of life. As my spiritual mother once said, "I didn't wait till I had a physical struggle to learn how to pray prayers of healing. I knew them, I meditated on them, and when I needed them; they were there." There is wisdom in learning how to pray, what to pray, and when to pray. Use this as a starting point, a guide to give you direction, but when the words of the prayer run out; allow your heart to flow out freely before your Father.

I pray an impartation of boldness and supernatural faith over you right now in Jesus name! I believe that you are going to discover a thirst for prayer that you've never known before. I believe The Lord, our God, wants to move mountains through your prayer life and it begins here. Most of the prayers have a corresponding Bible verse with them. I highly encourage you to open your bible and dive deep into the passage that correlates with your situation.

And remember, prayer isn't a one time thing; honey it's an all the time thing! You may pray one or many of these prayers over and over again. That is okay. Meditate on the verses given and allow God's word to change you and your situation from the inside out. I may not know you, but I love you. You're my sister in Christ and I am cheering you on. I pray you partner with what Holy Spirit is doing right now and help Him advance His Kingdom on this earth! Get to praying sister.

XOXO, Natalie

Anxiety

Jesus, I believe that You are my portion. Anxiety has no place in me. Restlessness and anxious thoughts will not be my daily reality. I am equipped and ready to deal with this once and for all. Holy Spirit I invite you to fill me with power to overcome. I command anxiety to go from my life, my family, my home, my work place, and ministry right now in Jesus name. I cancel this assignment against my life and declare I am hidden in the spirit. Anxiety will not find its way back to me. I walk in power, love, and a sound mind. Peace is my portion. Peace is my portion. Peace is my portion. In Jesus name, Amen.

Be anxious for nothing, but in everything by prayer and supplication, with thanksgiving, let your requests be made known to God." Philippians 4:6

Appetite

Jesus, I desire to walk in your ways. I am a real woman with a real appetite and that is okay. I pray for help to walk in portion control and healthy eating habits. I will not walk in emotional eating, binge eating, starvation or gluttony. I am walking strong in the Holy Spirit and I have control over my eating. Food will serve my body and health will be my portion. I rebuke all attacks on my health concerning food right now in Jesus name, Amen.

My food," said Jesus, "is to do the will of him who sent me and to finish his work. John 4:34

Ambition

Jesus, I have strong determination to complete Your will. I have ambition to be the best woman, wife, mother and Christian that I can be. I understand my goals and desires will take hard work and diligence. I believe You are pouring out what is necessary for me to complete my goals. You are guiding me Lord and I fully submit my ideas, plan and ways to You. Have your way in my desires and help maintain this strong desire to accomplish what you have set before me. I am being filled with the Holy Spirit to overflow in Jesus name, Amen.

The heart of man plans his way,but the Lord establishes his steps. Proverbs 16:9

Attitude
Jesus, ruin me for normal. I am not controlled by my attitude, my attitude is controlled by me, and I am led by the Holy Spirit. Emotions do not have the authority to determine my attitude or outlook on my life, situation or circumstances. My attitude is one of gratitude and joy. Joy is my portion. I will laugh in the Lord and have a pleasing outlook on my life. I command all pressing situations causing a poor attitude to be dealt with in the Spirit right now. I see the Lord pouring out a spirit of Praise upon me. I receive joy. I receive joy. I receive joy. Joy is my choice, in Jesus name, Amen.

Finally, brothers, whatever is true, whatever is honorable, whatever is just, whatever is pure, whatever is lovely, whatever is commendable, if there is any excellence, if there is anything worthy of praise, think about these things. What you have learned and received and heard and seen in me— practice these things, and the God of peace will be with you. Phillipians 4:8-9

Ashamed
Jesus, shame is not what You desire for my life and I refuse to walk in it a moment longer. Shame is not a part of disciple therefore it is not what You have for me. There is no

condemnation for those in Christ Jesus. Father I ask that You handle the situations causing me to feel ashamed and work them out for my good. I pray receiving confidence and assurance that I am loved, chosen, and set apart to do the will of God. I am not walking in the ways of the world. I rebuke shame and accusations brought against me by my adversary. Search me Lord and put within me a clean heart that is free from all bondage. Fill me with love for myself and others Holy Spirit. In Jesus name, Amen.

There is therefore now no condemnation for those who are in Christ Jesus. Romans 8:1

Afraid
Jesus, I was not given a spirit of fear, but a spirit of love, power and a sound mind. I will fear no evil. I will not fear or be in dismay by the season, the situation or the time. I know and trust that You are holding me in Your hand. You are working all these things out for my good even when I can't see that. I have faith that Holy Spirit has gone before me and I trust He is caring for this situation. I receive the power of the Holy Spirit which enables me to walk out of fear and into truth. Abba Father loves me and His will will be done in my life. I receive greater faith. In Jesus name, Amen.

I was not given a spirit of fear, but a spirit of love power and a sound mind. 2 Timothy 1:7

Apologize
Father, allow me to apologize when I need to. Help me to lay down my pride, ego and reputation and admit fault, especially in my marriage and relationships. I realize that I do not have to argue my point or explain why, if I am right, but I do have to reconcile humbly with those around me as it is Your will

Father. I receive the truth that apologizing and accepting fault is just as powerful for me as it is the other person. It sets me free from offense. Help me to forgive Lord. I rebuke bitterness, resentment and anger. It has no place in my life. I receive humility in Jesus name, Amen.

So if you are offering your gift at the altar and there remember that your brother has something against you, leave your gift there before the altar and go. First be reconciled to your brother, and then come and offer your gift. Matthew 5:23-24

Bar

Father, forgive me for the late nights, the wrongdoing and the ways of the world. I desire to please you Lord and I understand bad company corrupts good morals. Help me to resist temptation and be delivered from a lifestyle that you do not desire for me. Help me to forgive any pain that might cause me to turn to this lifestyle. Raise up friends around me that desire to live for you Lord. Remove people from my life that You did not put there and help me be brave enough to let them go. Erase my sins, my mistakes and make me a stable woman in the Lord. I praise you Holy Spirit for I know You are filling me up and helping me overcome sin once and for all. In Jesus name, Amen.

Do not be deceived: "Bad company ruins good morals." 1 Corinthians 15:33
Be sober-minded; be watchful. Your adversary the devil prowls around like a roaring lion, seeking someone to devour. 1 Peter 5:8

Beauty

Father, I receive beauty for ashes. All the sin, shame, and regretful mistakes that I have made do not define me or stop me from being beautiful in Your sight. I was made in the image of God therefore I am beautiful and filled with joy, laughter and love. I was made for such a time as this. My beauty comes from the Lord and not from the opinions or thoughts of the world or even people around me. I am not defined by clothing, make up, or my outward appearance. I am loved and I am beautiful. I will shine bright for the Lord. I will glow with the Presence of the Holy Spirit resting upon me. In Jesus name, Amen.

I will give them beauty for ashes. Isaiah 61:3

Bitter
Jesus, I admit that I am bitter. I admit that I have allowed this situation to set up a stronghold in my mind, but God I do not desire to walk in this even a moment longer. Holy Spirit come in and search my soul. Go to the very beginning of the wound and heal me Lord. I am willing to walk through healing with you Lord. I am willing to let this go, because I understand that bitterness is sin and I rebuke the root of bitterness in Jesus name. Forgive me Lord and forgive the person I am bitter towards. I speak blessings, peace and health over this person. I ask that You pour out your love upon them God. Free me from this bondage. I receive forgiveness, therefore, I give forgiveness. In Jesus name, Amen.

Strive for peace with everyone, and for the holiness without which no one will see the Lord. See to it that no one fails to obtain the grace of God; that no "root of bitterness" springs up and causes trouble, and by it many become defiled; Hebrews 12:14-15

Birth
Oh Jesus, how I praise You for the beautiful gift of life in my womb. I praise You for the gift You have graciously poured out. Bless this child, prosper them, and allow good health to be their potion. I will not walk in fear of pain or concern of the unknown. I walk boldly into the birthing process knowing that

my body was made and equipped to birth new life. Holy Spirit come and oversee the entire process. Bless my body, my womb and my child. Prepare us both for the birthing process. In Jesus name, Amen.

Vaginal Birth
Jesus, help me push, prepare my baby to come out of my womb easily and without resistance or strain. Cause everything to work out in favor of me and my child. Help me to stay calm and have a wonderful birthing experience. Holy Spirit be with us, the doctor, nurses and/or midwife. I declare that peace is my portion and my birthing experience will be wonderful. I speak health over myself and my child in Jesus name, Amen.

C Section
Jesus, thank you for modern medicine and its ability to help me birth my child even when my body/baby isn't able to do so the vaginally. I rebuke fear and declare this surgery is serving me and not hurting me. I pray for the doctors, nurses and staff. Holy Spirit guide their hands and prepare my body supernaturally for this surgery. I will heal quickly and without error. My child will be healthy and this procedure will be a good experience. I rebuke infection and the possibility of it. Heal my body quickly Lord. In Jesus name, Amen.

Behold, children are a heritage from the Lord, the fruit of the womb a reward.Like arrows in the hand of a warrior are the children of one's youth.Blessed is the man who fills his quiver with them! He shall not be put to shame when he speaks with his enemies in the gate. Psalm 127:3-5

Bold
Holy Spirit, cause boldness to come upon me suddenly. I declare the Lord's favor over my life and it causes me to speak boldly about the things of the Lord. I am not afraid to declare that Jesus Christ is Lord and He saved me from eternal separation from the Father. I am bold to use every platform I have to speak of the Lord's goodness, including my

home, my family, social media, my coworkers, my fellow church members and any other area I have access to reach people. I will speak boldly of what The Lord has done. I will share my testimony! I will speak the truth of scripture. In Jesus name, Amen.

Since we have such a hope, we are very bold 2 Corinthians 3:12

Bossy
Calm down boss babe. It doesn't always have to be your way.

Jesus, I release full control of my life, the people in my life and the situations around me to you. I repent of being bossy, pushy and even manipulative to get my way. Help me understand and accept the ideas, thoughts and opinions of others. While the opinions of others do not define me and I do not have to like them, I also don't have to change them. I do not desire to control the people around me and I pray that you would help me with that desire when it rises up. Holy Spirit fill me with love for others and open my eyes to see Your greatness in the lives of people around me. I rebuke the lie that has taken root to cause me to become bossy. I rebuke a controlling spirit and declare that I am led by the Spirit of God. In Jesus name, Amen.

Blessed are the pure in heart, for they shall see God. Matthew 5:8

Busy
If the enemy can't keep you in sin, he will just keep you busy.

Jesus, I repent of the lie that I am too busy to serve you, attend church, or accomplish the things You have asked of me. I am able to love my family well, I am diligent in prayer, and I can regularly attend church. Help me understand that I do have time for what I make a priority and that what the world says are my top priorities is false. My top priorities are You, my family and accomplishing Your will. I can say no, I can cut back on my schedule and I do not have to say yes to everything that comes in front of me. Holy Spirit come and open my heart to see what I need to remove from my life immediately. I repent of not putting You first Lord. In Jesus name, Amen.

Now as they went on their way, Jesus entered a village. And a woman named Martha welcomed him into her house. And she had a sister called Mary, who sat at the Lord's feet and listened to his teaching. But Martha was distracted with much serving. And she went up to him and said, "Lord, do you not care that my sister has left me to serve alone? Tell her then to help me." But the Lord answered her, "Martha, Martha, you are anxious and troubled about many things, but one thing is necessary. Mary has chosen the good portion, which will not be taken away from her." Luke 10:38-42

Boring

Jesus, ruin me for normal, break my heart and quicken my feet to run from "status quo Christianity". I was not saved and set free from so much to live a life without seeing supernatural movement of the Holy Spirit. Holy Spirit equip me to go make disciples of nations. Baptize me with fire to see the miraculous on this earth. Lord I want to see blind eyes open, deaf ears hear and the sick be healed. If You can use anyone, use me Lord. I refuse to be a pew sitter or one who is always poured into, but never pours out. I am stepping into the miracle working realm and I AM moving in the things of God. In Jesus name, Amen.

Truly, truly, I say to you, whoever believes in me will also do the works that I do; and greater works than these will he do, because I am going to the Father. John 14:12

Calm

Jesus, I am calm and not easily alarmed. I am level headed. I am not quick to anger. I choose my thoughts and words wisely. I understand that it is my choice to be moved by my circumstances and I do not have to be run my emotions. I am not an emotional or uptight person. I am calm and breath easy knowing the Lord orders my steps. In Jesus name, Amen.

Trust in the Lord with all your heart, and do not lean on your own understanding. In all your ways acknowledge him, and he will make straight your paths. Proverbs 3:5-6

Callous
Jesus, help me to be sensitive and caring to other people. Remove the thick hardness that I have allowed to surround me and soften my heart. Help me be open with people and allow them to love me. Holy Spirit go to the root of what has caused this and heal me. Reveal to me what has caused me to get to this place and remove the scales from my eyes. Father I believe You love me and I will begin walking in that love. In Jesus name, Amen.

They have become callous and have given themselves up to sensuality, greedy to practice every kind of impurity. But that is not the way you learned Christ!— assuming that you have heard about him and were taught in him, as the truth is in Jesus, to put off your old self,which belongs to your former manner of life and is corrupt through deceitful desires. Ephesians 4:19-22

Captive
Jesus, set me free from myself, from the opinions of others and from the snares of the enemy. Break the chains that are wrapped around my spirit, soul and flesh. Holy Spirit fill me up with Your freedom and help me embrace the truth of who I am. I am no longer a slave to sin, I am a child of God. I will no longer walk bound by the ways of this world. I am set free to live for the one who gave it all for me. In Jesus name, Amen.

The Spirit of the Lord God is upon me, because the Lord has anointed me to bring good news to the poor; he has sent me to bind up the brokenhearted, to proclaim liberty to the captives, and the opening of the prison to those who are bound; Isaiah 61:1

Catty

Jesus, I repent of being deliberately hurtful in my words and actions toward others. Forgive me of being spiteful and allowing bitterness to flow onto others threw me. I don't take this attitude lightly and I realize it is not Your will for your life. Repair the relationships I have damaged due to this way of thinking and help me to regain favor with those in my life. Holy Spirit baptize me with fire. Lead me, set me free, and raise me up to be an example for other women. In Jesus name, Amen.

For those who live according to the flesh set their minds on the things of the flesh, but those who live according to the Spirit set their minds on the things of the Spirit. For to set the mind on the flesh is death, but to set the mindon the Spirit is life and peace. Romans 8:5-6

Children

Jesus, bless my children, protect them, give them good health, and allow them to walk in Your ways all the days of their life. Help me to raise them the way You desire. I believe they will not depart from You. I rebuke all attacks of the enemy over their life and I declare favor and spiritual maturity will be their portion. Holy Spirit I know You are not bound by time so I ask that You go into their tomorrow and work all things out for their good. Help me to nurture the God given gifts, talents, and disposition You gave them Lord. Lead me in leading my children. In Jesus name, Amen.

Train up a child in the way he should go; even when he is old he will not depart from it. Proverbs 22:6

Compulsive

Jesus, help me restrain from compulsive and poor decisions, especially in the area of my finances. Help me to show maturity and wisdom in all my decisions. I invite Holy Spirit to lead me in this area and convict me when I am making poor choices. I praise You Lord for You give wisdom to those who ask. Pour out Your wisdom upon me that I might walk in Your ways Lord. Undo all the damage I have caused because of my lack of control. I trust that as I repent You are working all things out for my good Lord. In Jesus name, Amen.

But I say, walk by the Spirit, and you will not gratify the desires of the flesh. For the desires of the flesh are against the Spirit, and the desires of the Spirit are against the flesh, for these are opposed to each other, to keep you from doing the things you want to do. Galatians 5:16-17

Conceive

Father, I cry out before You believing that You hear me, trusting You will answer me and walking in faith that You are overseeing everything concerning me. Open my womb Lord. Put within me a child that I may bare fruit from my womb. Prepare myself and my husband to receive this beautiful gift of life. I believe Your word and You said if I ask anything in your name, You will do it for me. In Jesus name, Amen.

It came about in due time, after Hannah had conceived, that she gave birth to a son; and she named him Samuel, saying, "Because I have asked him of the LORD." 1 Samuel 1:20

Condescending

Holy Spirit, I repent of being led by a prideful spirit and I bind it up right now in Jesus name. I loose the glory of God and I fully submit myself to You alone God. I pray you would forgive me of operating in the flesh and teach me how to surrender my own desires for Yours. Lord I am not better than others and I repent of thinking more highly of myself than I ought. I humble myself before you and declare that I will operate in love toward everyone around me. In Jesus name, Amen.

And as you wish that others would do to you, do so to them. Luke 6:31

Confusion

Jesus, I know You are not a God of confusion and you do not cause confusion. I rebuke confusion and command it to go in Jesus name. I receive clarity of mind right now in Jesus name. Jesus Your word says You are the King of Peace and I know that You will always lead me with Your peace. I pray that you bestow Your perfect peace upon me and illuminate what choice I need to make. Help me follow Your peace. In Jesus name, Amen.

For God is not a God of confusion but of peace… 1 Corinthians 14:33

Cranky

Holy Spirit, it is so easy to give in to my flesh. It takes much less effort to be fully led by my flesh than to surrender my mind, will, and emotions and be led in a way contrary to my flesh. I declare and decree that I will no longer be controlled by my feelings or emotions. I take full responsibility for my behavior and attitude. I surrender it to you now Lord. If in fact this crackiness is being caused by some unknown issue, I pray You would reveal it to me now. In Jesus name, Amen.

You, however, are not in the flesh but in the Spirit, if in fact the Spirit of God dwells in you. Anyone who does not have the Spirit of Christ does not belong to him. But if Christ is in you, although the body is dead because of sin, the Spirit is life because of righteousness. If the Spirit of him who raised Jesus from the dead dwells in you, he who raised Christ Jesus from the dead will also give life to your mortal bodies through his Spirit who dwells in you. Romans 8:9-11

Church
If not in church…

Jesus, Your word calls me to be connected to a local church body. I repent of being offended, far away, and even angry at the church. I pray You would show me what church You have called me to be physically a part of. Holy Spirit I desire to have more of You in my life and I understand that more of You often times comes from being around people who live for you. I repent of my pride and I renounce the lie that I can do this alone. Lord I understand that I cannot do this alone and I will not spend another week without being surrounded by my spiritual family. I rebuke the enemy trying to keep me from the church I am called to and command it to go NOW in Jesus name. I loose the Power of The Holy Spirit to lead me and guide me. Jesus help me be a faithful church member, a servant in my church and a faithful tither as this is what Your word asks of me. In Jesus name, Amen.

not neglecting to meet together, as is the habit of some, but encouraging one another, and all the more as you see the Day drawing near. Hebrews 10:25

If in church...

Holy Spirit, I submit myself to You fully and I surrender my own will. Help me to be all that You have called me to be in the church. Show me where You are calling me to serve and give my time. Help me be obedient to give cheerfully, serve faithfully, and love with all my heart. I rebuke offense and I command it to go in Jesus name. I loose the glory of God over myself and my church. Teach me how to pray for my pastors and encourage them. I pray even now that Holy Spirit would supernaturally encourage and revive my pastor and his/her family. Lift any ill fitting burden that they are carrying off and bless them beyond their wildest dreams. Help me get connected Lord. In Jesus name, Amen.

The point is this: whoever sows sparingly will also reap sparingly, and whoever sows bountifully will also reap bountifully. Each one must give as he has decided in his heart, not reluctantly or under compulsion, for God loves a cheerful giver. 2 Corinthians 9:6-7

Deceitful

Holy Spirit, I repent of my sin! I command every lying and manipulating spirit that is hindering me, oppressing me and even possessing me to go NOW in Jesus name! I will not serve deceit. I will ONLY serve Jesus Christ. I pray now that my tongue would be loosed from wickness and I ask for tongues of fire to be my portion. Renew me Lord. Put within me a new heart with a new conviction. Make me aware of Your Presence Holy Spirit. In Jesus name, amen.

Lying lips are an abomination to the Lord, but those who act faithfully are his delight. Proverbs 12:22

Demanding

Lord, forgive me for poor attitudes of striving and strife. Put within me a new heart and help me to be fully led by You, Holy Spirit. Help me to realize that everything does not have to go the way I think it should and I am not always right. Humble me Lord. Make me like You. Help me walk in your holy ways. In Jesus name, amen.

Create in me a clean heart, O God, and renew a right spirit within me. Romans 51:10

Different

Holy Spirit, help me to truly love myself just the way I am. I receive by faith a new love for myself and how different I am. It is okay to be different! And Father, if You made me this way, I know that I am pretty special. Holy Spirit help me to truly understand that speaking against myself is speaking against the very One who created me. Help me love me the way You love me Lord. Help me see myself the way You see me Lord. Help me to remember that I am worth dying for. In Jesus name, amen.

I praise you, for I am fearfully and wonderfully made. Wonderful are your works; my soul knows it very well. Psalm 139:14

Detox
Holy Spirit, I feel You nudging me to detox certain people, places and things from my life. If I am not ready to let go, make me ready. I surrender my ideas, thoughts, and dreams to You Lord and I trust You're working all things out for my good. Holy Spirit guide me and help me lean into You more on a daily basis. I open the door for You to detox my life from all negativity and evil. I send it all away right now in the name of Jesus Christ. I want You and You alone God. In Jesus name, amen.

Since we have these promises, beloved, let us cleanse ourselves from every defilement of body and spirit, bringing holiness to completion in the fear of God. 2 Corinthians 7:1

Demon
There is no depth or height, no angel or demon, there is NOTHING that can separate me from The Love of God! I command ALL demons to GO NOW in the only name that can save, JESUS CHRIST! I break every word curse, every vex, hex, bewitchment and enchantment. I break every working of a curse, witchcraft, generational curses, and demonic soul ties right now in Jesus name. I repent of sin and wickedness.

Jesus Christ is my savior and only Him will I serve. I WILL NOT SERVE YOU SATAN! I WILL ONLY SERVE JESUS CHRIST! I close every demonic door that is open to my life. I command every person that is sent on assignment to advance hell in my life to GO in Jesus name. Harden their hearts Holy Spirit and help me to let them walk away. Holy Spirit come now and fill me up to overflow. Sweep this house, fill it, and put it back in order. I will walk in the ways of The Lord. I loose the power of the Holy Spirit and a renewed mind in Jesus name. Amen.

When an impure spirit comes out of a person, it goes through arid places seeking rest and does not find it. Then it says, 'I will return to the house I left. When it arrives, it finds the house swept clean and put in order. Luke 11:24-25

Depressed

Depression is not my portion and right now I receive by faith clarity of spirit and soul. I receive joy, everlasting joy that comes from heaven above. I receive joy that cannot be shaken by circumstances or situations. Holy Spirit pull me out of this. PULL ME OUT RIGHT NOW IN JESUS NAME. I WILL NOT, I CANNOT STAY HERE, AND TODAY I AM STEPPING OUT OF THIS. I submit my mind, will, and emotions to the power of God. I command everything hindering me to go in Jesus name. I loose the glory of God to fall heavily upon me right now. Come Holy Spirit and rest with me, minister to me and make me whole again. In Jesus name, amen. (See demon prayer)

Come to me, all who labor and are heavy laden, and I will give you rest. Take my yoke upon you, and learn from me, for I am gentle and lowly in heart, and you will find rest for your souls.

For my yoke is easy, and my burden is light." Matthew 11:28-30

Detached
Father, I feel separated and disconnected. It is as if I walk through the day feeling numb and unsure of why I can't truly connect the way I desire. I pray that right now in this very moment that I would feel and know the embrace of the Holy Spirit. I break the chains that are binding me and I loose the Presence of God to surround me. Holy Spirit, You're welcome into every area of my life. I humbly ask that You help me connect to my life and the people in it the way You desire me to. In Jesus name, amen.

Delight
Jesus, I desire to find my delight in You alone. I know that if I am struggling to read my Bible, attend church or participate in daily worship it is not because I have a discipline problem; it is because I have a delight problem. Lord when You are my delight I will not want nor will I be led astray by the passions of my flesh. I delight myself in You now Jesus; submitting myself fully to Your will and Your ways. Oh Holy Spirit come and take my hand and turn my eyes toward Christ every minute of every day. I desire to please You in all my ways Lord. In Jesus name, amen.

Delight yourself in the Lord, and he will give you the desires of your heart. Psalm 37:4

Divine
Holy Spirit, help me to know what is divinely inspired by You and what is a counterfeit bidding for my attention. I repent of calling things Holy that are not. Give me eyes to see and ears to hear that I may know the perfect and acceptable will of God.

I ask to receive the gift of discernment right now in Jesus name. Help me to navigate this gifting and walk in it with Your Power. Surround me with people who love you and move in the power of You, Holy Spirit. In Jesus name, amen.

Do not be conformed to this world, but be transformed by the renewal of your mind, that by testing you may discern what is the will of God, what is good and acceptable and perfect. Romans 12:2

Emotional

Jesus, when You died You paid the price for all sin and the effects of it. You did not just die to get me into heaven, You died to get heaven into me. I accept and receive that perfect peace right now in Jesus name. I am not an emotional person who is run by every whim of emotion. Emotions change, but Your steadfast love endures forever and that is what I will put my trust in. I repent of being led by my flesh, my will and my emotions. I receive by faith the power of The Holy Spirit that helps me overcome. I command every demonic spirit coming against me, oppressing me or possessing me to GO NOW IN JESUS NAME. I loose the glory of God! Freedom is my portion. In Jesus name, amen.

But I say, walk by the Spirit, and you will not gratify the desires of the flesh. Galatians 5:16

Empowered

Because of Jesus' sacrifice and the outpouring of the Holy Spirit I am empowered to overcome sin. Sin has no dominion over me. I receive by faith the power of The Holy Spirit right now in Jesus name. I have been empowered by God to advance His Kingdom on this earth and I will not take this assignment lightly. Holy Spirit move in my life and open my eyes to how You want to move through me. Show me and put people around me who will teach me Your ways. In Jesus name, amen.

But you will receive power when the Holy Spirit has come upon you, and you will be my witnesses in Jerusalem and in all Judea and Samaria, and to the end of the earth." Acts 1:8

Energy/Exhausted

Father, You did not design me to be constantly exhausted and lethargic. You created me in Your image and have given me supernatural power from the Holy Spirit. I repent of not taking a Sabbath weekly. Birth within me a deep conviction to obey Your commands. You created the heavens and the earth and everything in it in six days, but on the seventh day You rested. Oh how much more do I need rest if You do, Lord? I pray that through my obedience and repentance energy would be restored back to my physical body. I rebuke and break off mental fatigue, sickness due to a lack of rest, exhaustion and mental issues stemming from over exertion of energy. I receive restoration in every area of my life. In Jesus name, amen.

Remember the Sabbath day, to keep it holy. Six days you shall labor, and do all your work, but the seventh day is a Sabbath to the Lordyour God. On it you shall not do any work, you, or your son, or your daughter, your male servant, or your female servant, or your livestock, or the sojourner who is within your gates. For in six days the Lordmade heaven and earth, the sea, and all that is in them, and rested on the seventh day. Therefore the Lord blessed the Sabbath day and made it holy. Exodus 20:8-11

Embarrassed

Father, help me to see myself the way You see me. Help to overcome the constant need to think and rethink about what I said and did. I rebuke tormenting spirits right now in Jesus name. I loose the truth of Christ over my life. I am free from the opinions of others and I refuse to view myself through the lense of my mistakes. I am free and I will only view myself through the lense of Christ. In Jesus name, amen.

For you have died, and your life is hidden with Christ in God. Colossians 3:13

Empty

Oh Jesus, fill me Lord. From the tips of my toes to the crown of my head. Fill me with Your love the truth of Your word. Help me to overflow with Your love and power. Show me who You say I am. Fill me up with Your Spirit God. In Jesus name, amen.

And they were all filled with the Holy Spirit and began to speak with other tongues, as the Spirit was giving them utterance. Acts 2:4

Fake

I refuse to be fake with myself and with others. Holy Spirit, open my eyes to areas where I pretend to be someone or something that I am not. I command any deceptive spirit that is trying to have a place in my life to go in Jesus name. I receive total freedom from the opinions of others. I do not have to be someone else. I can be totally loved just as I am. In Jesus name, amen.

So put away all malice and all deceit and hypocrisy and envy and all slander. 1 Peter 2:2

Faith

Jesus, I received my precious salvation by faith and I now ask that You help me live my entire life by faith. Faith to do what You have asked of me. Faith to take risks You're asking me to take. Faith to live the way You have called me to even if it looks different. Faith to know You're working everything out for my good. I ask to receive the supernatural gift of faith. Teach me how to operate in this precious gift. In Jesus name, amen.

He said to them, "Because of your little faith. For truly, I say to you, if you have faith like a grain of mustard seed, you will say to this mountain, 'Move from here to there,' and it will move, and nothing will be impossible for you." Matthew 17:20

Fierce

Jesus, You have called me to be as wise as a serpent and as innocent as a dove. I refuse to be timid about my faith and its life changing impact. I rebuke every demonic spirit trying to shut me up! I will proclaim from the rooftops what You have done for me, Lord. Help me to be fierce in my pursuit of holiness and burn out sin within me. I want to burn bright like a blazing fire for You Lord. In Jesus name, amen.

Behold, I am sending you out as sheep in the midst of wolves, so be wise as serpents and innocent as doves. Matthew 10:16

Frustrated

Father, things don't look the way I thought they would, but I trust you. I am frustrated by my situation and circumstances, but I trust You. I want the very earth to witness me say, "I TRUST YOU!" I want to hear myself say, "I TRUST YOU!" I put my trust in You Christ. I will not be shaken. Regardless of how this goes, I trust You. I ask that You give me peace that surpasses understanding. In Jesus name, amen.

Be angry and do not sin; do not let the sun go down on your anger, Ephesians 4:26

Funny

Holy Spirit, You aren't a prude and I don't want to be either. You aren't boring or afraid of a big personality. Help me to find humor in even the little things in life for I know laughter is a good medicine. Help me to laugh all day long and boast in the goodness of my King. I love you, Lord. I love Your creative and loving personality. I pray I reflect You. In Jesus name, amen.

So God created man in his own image, in the image of God he created him; male and female he created them. Genesis 1:27

Frantic

Holy Spirit, give me peace! Help me to calm down. I invite you to move in my life. I do not want to be led by frantic emotion or fear. I want to be led by You alone God. I repent of giving into my flesh and I ask to receive the fullness of You, Holy Spirit. Baptize me in fire. In Jesus name, amen.

And the peace of God, which surpasses all understanding, will guard your hearts and your minds in Christ Jesus. Philippians 4:7

Friend

Jesus, You no longer call me a slave, but a friend. Help me to be a friend to others just as You have been a selfless friend to me. You gave up everything, so that You and I could be friends. I see in this just how important friendship is to You. Help me to love my friends, serve them and be a light for You in their lives. I also pray that You would bring Godly friends into my life. I pray for friends that love you, Lord. Friends that will further the calling of God on my life and not take away from it. Lord as scary as this sounds, I ask that You remove all "friends" that You did not put in my life. Help me be brave and let them leave. In Jesus name, amen.

No longer do I call you servants, for the servant does not know what his master is doing; but I have called you friends, for all that I have heard from my Father I have made known to you.
John 15:15

Forgive

Father, You have forgiven me of my sin because of Jesus' perfect sacrifice. I have been cleansed by the blood of Jesus and I am now a child of God. Lord, I want to be like You in all my ways. I know not everything You did for me was easy or felt good, but nonetheless You did it. Help me to live that way God. Help me to forgive even when it hurts. Help me to love the unlovable and serve the least of these. Forgive me for my unforgiveness and help me repent immediately. In Jesus name, amen.

For if you forgive other people when they sin against you, your heavenly Father will also forgive you. But if you do not forgive others their sins, your Father will not forgive your sins.
Matthew 6:14-15

Fire

Holy Spirit, when You were poured out onto this earth You did not come quietly. You came like a mighty rushing wind and appeared as tongues of fire to those who were waiting for You. John the Baptist prophesied of You when He said, "The one who is coming after me will baptize You in fire." I may not fully understand what that means or looks like, but if it's You; I want it. All of me wants all of you. Come now and baptize me

Holy Spirit. Baptize me in fire from on high. Put within me every good gift and surround me with people who will cultivate this flame in my life. I repent of false teaching. I want all of You God. In Jesus name, amen.

for our God is a consuming fire. Hebrews 12:29

Gifted

Holy Spirit, You give good gifts and I desire to walk in those. I know that The Word of God says that You will distribute as You will good gifts to those who ask and I ask to receive everything You desire for me to have right now in Jesus name. Help me to walk in these gifts and steward them in a manner worthy of Your name. Help me to host Your Presence Holy Spirit. Surround me with people who will teach me, train me, and equip me to use these gifts to advance Your Kingdom. In Jesus name, amen.

Now there are varieties of gifts, but the same Spirit; and there are varieties of service, but the same Lord; and there are varieties of activities, but it is the same God who empowers them all in everyone. To each is given the manifestation of the Spirit for the common good. For to one is given through the Spirit the utterance of wisdom, and to another the utterance of knowledge according to the same Spirit, to another faith by the same Spirit, to another gifts of healing by the one Spirit, to another the working of miracles, to another prophecy, to another the ability to distinguish between spirits, to another various kinds of tongues, to another the interpretation of tongues. All these are empowered by one and the same Spirit, who apportions to each one individually as he wills. 1 Corinthians 12:4-11

Generous

Father, You love a cheerful giver, not one who gives out of compulsion or reluctancy. I know where my money is there my heart will be also. Open my eyes to see where You want me to give generously. Malachi 3:10 tells me that You expect me to give 10% of all my earnings to my local church, but I understand that is just the beginning of generosity. That same verse says I should be faithful with my offerings as well. Show me where You want me to give and help me to be faithful to do it, Lord. Remind me to pay for the person behind me in line and help those around me who are in need. If You can use anyone, use me Lord. In Jesus name, amen.

Whoever is generous to the poor lends to the LORD, and he will repay him for his deed. Proverbs 19:17

Glam
Father, I pray when people see me they see You. I praise You for my outward appearance for I know I am made in Your image, but I pray that above all I would carry Your glory. Use me, all of me, to advance Your Kingdom God. I pray that because people know and see me, they come to know and see You. In Jesus name, amen.

to grant to those who mourn in Zion—to give them a beautiful headdress instead of ashes, the oil of gladness instead of mourning, the garment of praise instead of a faint spirit; that they may be called oaks of righteousness, the planting of the Lord, that he may be glorified. Isaiah 61:3

Grace
Jesus, You have given me great grace. You have given me unmerited favor that I do not deserve. You have shown me grace in situations where I should have received the due penalty for my shortcomings and mistakes. Yet, You forgive

me and showed me perfect grace. Help me to show that to others. Help me give grace to those around me. Help me realize that I do not have to be perfect and neither does everyone around. Please help me also have grace for myself. In Jesus name, amen.

For by grace you have been saved through faith. And this is not your own doing; it is the gift of God, not a result of works, so that no one may boast. Esphesians 2:8-9

Goals
Lord, I pray You help me turn my dreams to goals and my wishes to clear vision. I open the door for Holy Spirit to birth perfect dreams and visions inside me. Put within me Your goals for my life Lord. Help me be fierce and bold to pursue what You have called me to. I pray the goals that I am pursuing will bless those around me and make a meaningful impact for Your Kingdom. Let heaven come, Your will be done on earth as it is in heaven. Help me rest on the Sabbath, even if I want to keep working. Breathe on my efforts and do more than my wildest dreams! In Jesus name, amen.

Delight yourself in the LORD, and he will give you the desires of your heart. Proverbs 37:4

Gullible
Holy Spirit, You are the great teacher and The Word of God says You will teach me in all things. I know that I am kind of gullible or as some would say, "a little blonde", but that does not define me. I pray You would use this childlike faith to advance Your Kingdom. Heal me from believing the lie that I am always the joke. In Jesus name, amen.

But the Helper, the Holy Spirit, whom the Father will send in my name, he will teach you all things and bring to your remembrance all that I have said to you. John 14:26

Gossip

Father, I repent. Lord, help me to not be that woman. A woman that no one can truly trust, because of loose lips. Seal my lips with trust God and seal my heart with You, Holy Spirit. Undo everything I have done in the spirit through gossip and convict me strongly, if I begin to venture down that road. I pray for tongues of fire to fall upon me right now in Jesus name. I submit this unruly tongue to You. And Holy Spirit, even in those one on one settings where I think I can trust that person with everything; even then, please convict me. Show me the reality of what I am doing when I gossip about people. Remove people from my life who gossip and help me forgive those who gossip about me. In Jesus name, amen.

Let no corrupting talk come out of your mouths, but only such as is good for building up, as fits the occasion, that it may give grace to those who hear. Ephesians 4:29

Greed

Oh Holy Spirit, I repent! I rebuke greed right now in Jesus name and I command it to GO! I refuse to be led by greed or overcome by the love of money. The Word of God says I cannot serve God and money. So I declare right now by the power of the Holy Spirit I will not serve you, greed! I will only serve Jesus Christ. Help me give. Unclench my first, Lord and help me to give without measure. Help me give until greed is totally broken from my mind. In Jesus name, amen.

For the love of money is a root of all kinds of evils. It is through this craving that some have wandered away from the faith and pierced themselves with many pangs. 1 Timothy 6:10

Harsh

Jesus, You are never harsh with me. You speak to me through love every time You speak. I repent of being harsh and harming others with my words. Help me realize the impact my words have and use them to nourish the people around me. Help me to mend the relationships that I have damaged with my mouth. Use me, Lord. Use my tongue to glorify You. May my life sing of Your goodness. In Jesus name, amen.

A soft answer turns away wrath, but a harsh word stirs up anger. Proverbs 15:1

Hateful

Holy Spirit, a fruit of You is love, therefore, if I am using a hateful tone with my actions, demeanor or voice; I am not moving in You. I desire to glorify You with every single bit of my life. Forgive me, Lord. I repent of being fueled by selfish desires and for even being careless in how I treat other people. Help those I have hurt forgive me, help me to forgive them, and help me to forgive myself. I desire to move in Your power, not my own. In Jesus name, amen.

A gentle tongue is a tree of life, but perverseness in it breaks the spirit. Proverbs 15:4

Heaven

Oh Jesus, You did not die to just get me into heaven, You died to get heaven into me! So let heaven come. Your will be done on earth as it is in heaven. Oh I can hear it now, Lord, the sound of heaven touching earth. Come now Holy Spirit and invade my life. Invade my work place, my home, my marriage, my children, my church, my friendships and my mind. Use me to release heaven on this earth. I pray that when people enter into my presence they enter into Your Presence, because You overshadow every place of my life. In Jesus name, amen.

Pray then like this: "Our Father in heaven, hallowed be your name. Your kingdom come, your will be done, on earth as it is in heaven. Give us this day our daily bread, and forgive us our debts, as we also have forgiven our debtors. And lead us not into temptation, but deliver us from evil. Matthew 6:9-13 ESV

Healing
Jesus, You are the great physician. I will live by faith and not by sight. By Your stripes I was made well. I receive complete and total healing in my body right now in Jesus name. I rebuke the spirit of infirmity and command it to go right now! I loose the healing power of God to flow from the top of my head to the tips of my toes. Thank you Jesus for baring my burden, so I may be healed. I love You, Lord. Open my eyes to any changes I need to make to maintain the healing You have given me. In Jesus name, amen.

He Himself bore our sins in His own body on the tree, that we, being dead to sins, should live unto righteousness. "By His wounds you were healed." For you were as sheep going astray, but now have been returned to the Shepherd and Guardian of your souls. 1 Peter 2:24-25

Help
Jesus, You're my ever present help. You're my defender in time of need. I will look unto the hill for I see where my help comes from. My help comes from The Lord, the maker of heaven and earth. I will not look to my left or to my right for my

help for I know the one who created everything is working all things out for my good. I do not have to cry out as a servant begging a master. Oh no Lord, I call unto You as a child. As a daughter who trusts her Father. One who knows and believes. You are my helper Lord and in You alone I trust. In Jesus name, amen.

I lift up my eyes to the hills. From where does my help come? My help comes from the Lord, who made heaven and earth. Psalm 121:1-2

High
Father, You did not create me to live high. You did not create me to depend upon drugs, alcohol, or any other substance. You created me to depend upon You. I repent for the use of anything that made/makes me high. I rebuke the spirit of addiction and I command you to go right now in Jesus mighty name. I will not chase a high, but I will obey the Lord. I pray to receive the baptism of the Holy Spirit right now. Oh God, fill me with power from on high that I may overcome this once and for all. I pray that You would remove every person in my life who does not point me to you. Help me say NO, Lord. In Jesus name, amen.

Hey girl. You can do this, okay? I did it. I am no one special, just a woman just like you. I am cheering you on. I believe in you. Keep praying these prayers. Keep going to church. Keep loving your babies as best you can. You've got this sister. You're going to come out of this a new person. You are free, in Jesus name. I love you. XO-Nat

For freedom Christ has set us free; stand firm therefore, and do not submit again to a yoke of slavery. Galatians 5:1

Home

Holy Spirit, invade my home. Have Your way in the life of my family. I pray right now over every crossbeam, every board, every nail, every doorway, every bed, every piece of clothing, every piece of silverware and everything in between. I pray a blessing of The Lord be upon it. Not an earthly blessing, but a heavenly one. I pray for the blessing of Your Presence upon my home. I dedicate my home to You, God and I command every unclean spirit that may be in it go right now in Jesus name. My husband and I will walk in peace, my children will walk in the ways of the Lord, and in my home there will be no wants for The Lord our God has supplied all our needs. Oh God, come and inhabit our home. Establish Your throne upon the praises of our hearts. May everyone who enters this home immediately know, The Lord is here. In Jesus name, amen.

By wisdom a house is built, and by understanding it is established; by knowledge the rooms are filled with all precious and pleasant riches. Proverbs 24:3-4

Hothead

Holy Spirit, I submit my temper to You. I surrender the need to get angry over everything and completely lose my cool. I do not have to be that person. I rebuke generational curses. I will not be like my mother or father or anyone else in my family who operated out of wrath. I was given a Spirit of love, power and a sound mind. I do not have to get angry and lash out to communicate my feelings. Help me, Lord. Renew my mind and open my eyes to another way. In Jesus name, amen.

Be angry and do not sin; do not let the sun go down on your anger, Ephesians 4:26

Husband

Father, I pray for Your perfect will to be done in the life of my husband. I pray that You would help him to lead and guide this family just as You have created him to do. Help me to cheer him on in every aspect of life. Help me to love him as You have loved me. Remind me, daily, to remind him that he can do this. You created him to love and care for me, so I ask that you help me let him do just that. Forgive me, Father, for I know I fall short, but I pray that my shortcomings would not harm my husband. I love him, Lord. Oh how I love him. I pray that Holy Spirit would move in His heart and guide him into all truth. Help me to be his helpmate and allow him to lead even when I don't agree. Lead him, Lord. Pour out Your goodness, Your lavish love and You fresh anointing upon him. In Jesus name, amen.

Wives, submit to your husbands, as is fitting in the Lord. Husbands, love your wives, and do not be harsh with them. Colossians 3:18-19

Immature

Holy Spirit, I understand that maturity is not a fruit of Your Spirit, but it is a true mark of being in Your Presence and in Your word. I pray that You would help me to become the mature woman You created me to be. Help me make the right choices and help me be a beacon of hope for those around me. There is a time to grow up and I understand that will simply be a choice. I choose to do so, now, but only through Your Spirit. In Jesus name, amen.

But solid food is for the mature, for those who have their powers of discernment trained by constant practice to distinguish good from evil. Hebrews 5:14

Impatient

Holy Spirit, a fruit of Your Spirit is patience and if I am lacking in the fruits of the Spirit I am lacking in time with The Spirit. Help me to leverage the time that I already have; time in the car, when I am getting ready, doing laundry or cooking dinner. Help me become aware of Your Presence in those small moments. For I know that when I become aware of Your daily Presence I will walk in the fruits of Your Holy Spirit and that includes patience. In Jesus name, amen.

Rejoice in hope, be patient in tribulation, be constant in prayer. Romans 12:12

Innocent

Oh Father, protect my innocence in every meaning of the word. Protect me Father from anything that is falsely brought against me. Protect me from the temptations of this world and help me maintain the purity You've given me. Lord, speak on my behalf and go before me. Help me not to worry about what I will say for I know You will speak through me at the appointed time. I trust you God. In Jesus name, amen.

Do all things without grumbling or disputing, that you may be blameless and innocent, children of God without blemish in the midst of a crooked and twisted generation, among whom you shine as lights in the world, holding fast to the word of life, so that in the day of Christ I may be proud that I did not run in vain or labor in vain. Philippians 2:14-16

Inspire

Father, You are such a creative God. You created everything. The beautiful sky with perfect clouds, the beach with stunning sand and ocean waves and You are the brilliant one who told the water how far to go. You, My Father, You did that and Your Spirit lives within me. Inspire me to create, to feel and to move into action toward what You're calling me to. I pray for a creative anointing to rest upon me and an awareness of Holy Spirit every single day. Inspire me, God, for I know if I am inspired by You all my creations will glorify You. In Jesus name, amen.

For from him and through him and to him are all things. To him be glory forever. Amen. Romans 11:36

Israel

Oh Jesus, how precious are Your people. I pray for the Holy nation of Israel. I pray a blessing upon Your people and I pray for protection from all enemies. Increase them Lord, advance them in all their ways and prosper their land. Thank you Jesus for bridging the gap, so that I may become one of Your own. I pray for the land that You have called Holy. Remind me to pray for Israel, Holy Spirit. Thank you Lord, for allowing me to partner with Your will for Your people. In Jesus name, amen.

O Israel, trust in the LORD! He is their help and their shield. O house of Aaron, trust in the LORD! He is their help and their shield. Psalm 115:9-10

Indirect

Holy Spirit, help me to stop being indirect and expecting people to know what I am communicating. Forgive me for taking an offense when I did not directly state my expectations. Make me a bold person filled with You, Holy Spirit. Help to be brave and unashamed. Help to believe in myself the way You believe in me, Lord. In Jesus name, amen.

Jaded

Father, I know life has jaded me in some areas, but I open my life to You completely and I invite Holy Spirit to overflow into every area of my life. Make smooth the jagged pieces of my soul and put back together the broken places of my life. Help me to be vulnerable with the people who love me and help me to love them back. I desire to trust again, Lord and I believe You're helping me do that. In Jesus name, amen.

But for you who fear my name, the sun of righteousness shall rise with healing in its wings. You shall go out leaping like calves from the stall. Malachi 4:2

Jealous

Oh how deceitful jealousy is! Father, I am Your child and I have nothing to be jealous of. Help me, Lord. Help me to truly understand that when I celebrate the blessings of others I position my heart to receive the same, but when I am jealous and envious I completely stop the flow. I command jealousy to be broken off my life right now in the name of Jesus! I repent, I recieve forgiveness and today I commit to walking in joy toward others and their blessings. In Jesus name, amen.

But if you have bitter jealousy and selfish ambition in your hearts, do not boast and be false to the truth. This is not the wisdom that comes down from above, but is earthly, unspiritual, demonic. For where jealousy and selfish ambition exist, there will be disorder and every vile practice. James 3:14-16

Joy

Father, happiness comes from what happens, but joy comes from above. Joy is something I can choose to have in every season and every situation no matter what is going on. Joy is eternal and true joy brings with it the peace of heaven. I ask that my joy be fully restored right now in Jesus name. Please highlight the areas of my life that do not bring me joy and help me to either change or remove that from my life. I know that joy is my portion, because the joy of The Lord is my strength. I will receive strength when I walk in joy and I receive joy right now. In Jesus name, amen.

Then he said to them, "Go your way. Eat the fat and drink sweet wine and send portions to anyone who has nothing ready, for this day is holy to our Lord. And do not be grieved, for the joy of the Lord is your strength Nehemiah 8:10

Kind
Father, I know that Your goodness is what leads people to repentance and Your loving kindness draws those in need to You. I pray that I would be an extension of Your kindness on this earth. I pray that You would help me treat others with love, kindness and grace. Help me to be kind to everyone, including the people I don't agree with. In Jesus name, amen.

Love is patient, love is kind. It does not envy, it does not boast, it is not proud. It is not rude, it is not self-seeking, it is not easily angered, it keeps no record of wrongs. 1 Corinthians 13:4-5

Kiss
Father, You created me to be in a loving relationship with my husband. You have called me to love him and show love to him on a regular basis. I pray that You would ignite fire in our kiss and passion in our sex life. Give us eyes for one another and no one else. I rebuke lust and perversion and command it to go in Jesus name. I loose the truth of God over my marriage. I praise You, Holy Spirit for I know you are drawing

my husband and I closer together every single day. In Jesus name, amen.

Greet one another with a kiss of love Peace be to you all who are in Christ. 1 Peter 5:14

Karma

Jesus, Your work on the cross set me free from the law of reaping and sewing. Now I reap where I did not sew as a child of God and I do not receive the due penalty I deserve. I rebuke karma and I command any power that I have given it to be broken in Jesus name. I rebuke the spirit of witchcraft and command it go. I loose the spirit of truth over my life. I will not give credit either good or bad to this demonic alignment and I repent of acting in ignorance. In Jesus name, amen.

for the Lord knows the way of the righteous, but the way of the wicked will perish. Psalm 1:6

Kitchen

Jesus, I invite Your Holy Spirit to move mightily in my kitchen. I know the kitchen is the center of my home and it is where the nutrition of my family flows. I pray that You would open my eyes to foods and eating habits that do not serve my family. Help me to prepare healthy and blessed meals for my family. I pray that I would fall in love with serving my family. I pray that my eyes would be opened to the true blessing my kitchen is. I pray my kitchen would be a safe place for my family and friends to gather and encounter You. In Jesus name, amen.

She seeks wool and flax, and works with willing hands. She is like the ships of the merchant; she brings her food from afar. She rises while it is yet night and provides food for her household and portions for her maidens. Proverbs 31:13-15

Know It All

Holy Spirit, I confess I do not know everything, though sometimes I think I do. I pray that You would gently humble me and help to move when You say move and be quiet when You are quiet. Help me to deal with the "know it all's" in my life the way You want me to, with loving kindness. Help me to understand where they are coming from and help me to be a light in their life. In Jesus name, amen.

And I applied my heart to know wisdom and to know madness and folly. I perceived that this also is but a striving after wind. Ecclesiastes 1:17

Late

Jesus, You are never late, You are always on time. I pray that You help me to be the same. Help me to truly realize that being late communicates my lack of honor for the meeting, place and situation. I desire to honor the people I have made commitments to. Help me to become a woman of my word. Thank You, Holy Spirit for guiding me. In Jesus name, amen.

Do nothing from selfish ambition or conceit, but in humility count others more significant than yourselves. Philippians 2:3

Light

Jesus, You have called me to be the light of the world. I rebuke darkness from my life right now in Jesus name. Darkness has no authority or dominion over my life and I command it to go. I will walk in the light and I will be a light to the world. I will let the light of Jesus shine bright in every choice I make. Thank you for allowing me to partner with Your perfect will and advance Your Kingdom on this earth. In Jesus name, amen.

You are the light of the world. A city set on a hill cannot be hidden. Nor do people light a lamp and put it under a basket, but on a stand, and it gives light to all in the house. In the same way, let your light shine before others, so that they may see your good works and give glory to your Father who is in heaven. Matthew 5:14-16

Love

Oh what a lavish love that I should be called a child of God. Father, I praise You for Your love. Your love was so great for me You sent Your only begotten Son to die and rise again, for me. Your love was so strong it raised Jesus from the grave and enabled me to become Your daughter. I am wrecked by the thought of Your great love for me. Oh Lord, help that love overflow into every area of my life. I pray that my life would be a picture of Your love. In Jesus name, amen.

See what kind of love the Father has given to us, that we should be called children of God; and so we are. 1 John 3:1

Logic

Jesus, I praise You for logic and the ability to think and reason. I do, however, understand that Holy Spirit is not on the earth to serve my logic. Help me to lay down logic and reasoning when it hinders Holy Spirit from moving in my life. Help me to be a strong daughter full of discernment and good character. Use my knowledge, logic and reasoning to advance Your Kingdom, but help me know when it is time to lay logic down and operate in faith. In Jesus name, amen.

When I was a child, I spoke like a child, I thought like a child, I reasoned like a child. When I became a man, I gave up childish ways. 1 Corinthians 13:11

Loyal

Jesus, You are the most loyal of friends. You never leave me nor forsake me. You watch out for every area of my life and You intercede on my behalf day and night. I pray that I will be likewise, just as loyal to You, my church and the divine relationships You have placed into my life. Heal me of deep trust issues that stop me from being loyal to those You've placed in my life. In Jesus name, amen.

A friend loves at all times, and a brother is born for adversity. Proverbs 17:17

Lonely

Holy Spirit, You are always with me. I never have to be lonely, because I am in fact never alone. Help me to become aware of Your Presence. Help me to know Your embrace and discern when You have entered room. I pray even now that You would show up mightily in a profound way. I pray that I would feel Your warm hug and Presence all around me. Thank You for always being with me, Lord. In Jesus name, amen.

I will not leave you as orphans; I will come to you. John 14:18

Mad

Holy Spirit, I know that anger is not sin, but I also know The Word says when I am angry not to sin. If my anger has led me into sin, please forgive me. The Word says that the anger of man does not produce the righteousness of God. Help me to lay down my anger toward others and walk in true freedom. Help me to overcome this emotion right now and submit fully to the leading of the Holy Spirit. Thank you Lord! In Jesus name, amen.

My beloved brothers, understand this: Everyone should be quick to listen, slow to speak, and slow to anger, for man's anger does not bring about the righteousness that God desires. James 19-20

Manipulate

Holy Spirit, I repent of being led by the spirit of witchcraft. The scripture says that maniplutation if a form of witchcraft and it is rooted in deception. Convict me in deceptive behaviors and break my heart for what breaks Yours. Open my eyes to see the true magnitude of what is happening when people behave this way. I rebuke witchcraft and I command it go right now in Jesus name. I will not serve witchcraft or my flesh. I loose the glory of God to fill this room. I pray to receive a fresh baptism of Holy Spirit right now in Jesus name. Fill me up to overflow. In Jesus name, amen.

For rebellion is as the sin of divination, and presumption is as iniquity and idolatry. Because you have rejected the word of the LORD, he has also rejected you from being king." 1 Samuel 15:23

Maternal

Father, You are perfect in all Your ways. You are caring, gentle and loving toward me. I pray right now in Jesus name that I, too, would carry those attributes as I am made in Your image. Make my maternal instincts strong and help me to be motivated by love toward and for my children. Help me to forgive myself when I fall short and humble me when I think I've got it all figured out. I just desire to be an exceptional mother, one who pleases You in the way I raise my children. Help me show them You every single day. In Jesus name, amen.

Her children rise up and call her blessed; her husband also, and he praises her: Proverbs 31:28

Marriage

Holy Spirit, I commit this marriage into Your hands. This is the way You have chosen to show Your most precious covenant on this earth, through marriage between one man and one woman. I ask for Your precious and powerful Presence to motivate my marriage to be all You have called us to be. Help me to respect my husband and help my husband to love me. Use us to bring out the best in each other and equip us to help each other fulfill the calling of God on our lives. We love You, Lord and we say this marriage is Yours. Have Your perfect way and will in our lives. In Jesus name, amen.

Set me as a seal upon your heart, as a seal upon your arm, for love is strong as death, jealousy is fierce as the grave. Its flashes are flashes of fire, the very flame of the LORD. Many waters cannot quench love, neither can floods drown it. If a man offered for love all the wealth of his house, he would be utterly despised. Song of Solomon 8:6-7 MEV

Messy

Jesus, sometimes life gets messy. I know You are well aware of this as You walked this earth just as I do. Help me not to muddy the waters, but rather help me easily know wrong from right. Help me clean up my life in every area. Help me clean up my home, my work space, my car, and everything in between. While cleanliness is not next to Godliness, it sure helps to have a clean space to dwell in. So I ask for the supernatural help of Holy Spirit to accomplish this task. In Jesus name, amen.

Create in me a clean heart, O God, and renew a right spirit within me Psalm 51:10 MEV

Money

Jesus, You came to give me life and life more abundantly. You do not desire for me to struggle or live in poverty, but You also do not desire for me to be ran by the love of money. I pray that I will be delivered from the love of money and I rebuke the spirit of mammon. I command it go to in Jesus name. I loose the Spirit of God over my life. I pray the promise of Deuteronomy 8:18 over my life. You give the power to get wealth. I pray that You would release that power in my life and I pray that You would use my wealth to advance Your Kingdom. In Jesus name, amen. (Also see Poverty)

But you must remember the Lord your God, for it is He who gives you the ability to get wealth, so that He may establish His covenant which He swore to your fathers, as it is today Deuteronomy 8:18 MEV

Moving

Jesus, I commit this move into Your hands. I pray that You would lead every single part of this process. Calm my nerves and help me operate in wisdom. I pray that You would help me pack, throw out what needs to be thrown out, and give what I no longer need. Help me organize this the best way possible and use this move to glorify Your name. I pray this move would bless my family and serve them well. In Jesus name, amen. (Also see Home)

To everything there is a season, a time for every purpose under heaven: Ecclesiastes 3:1 MEV

Moody

Father, You created me as an emotional being. I feel and experience things as a woman that men simply cannot understand. You created me with the ability to have a cycle and bare children. I commit all of that in Your hands reminding You that You created me this way, not to harm me, but to serve Your perfect plan. I pray that You would help me manage my mood and emotions on a regular basis. I love You, Lord and my deepest desire is to serve You well with my life. In Jesus name, amen.

A fool gives full vent to his spirit, but a wise man quietly holds it back. Proverbs 29:11 MEV

No

Holy Spirit, give me boldness! It is okay to say no. I do not have to say yes to everything and I am receiving supernatural help to overcome this right now in Jesus name. Help me not be swayed by the opinions or emotions of others. Help me to do what is best for my faith, my family and myself; above all I want to do Your will Father. So help me to know when You're leading me to say yes and when You're leading me to say no. Help me to stand firm! In Jesus name, amen. (Also see Opinions)

But let your 'Yes' mean 'Yes,' and 'No' mean 'No.' For whatever is more than these comes from the evil one. Matthew 5:37 MEV

Nag

Father, Your Word says that a nagging wife is like cancer to the bones. I do not desire to be cancer to the bones of my husband or anyone else for that matter. Help me to control my tongue and attitudes. I break every generational curse and every word curse that I myself have spoken. I ask for forgiveness and I repent of this poor mindset. I release blessing in place of every nagging word I have spoken. In Jesus name, amen.

It is better to dwell in a corner of the housetop than with a brawling woman in a wide house. Proverbs 21:9 MEV

Narcissistic

Father, I ask that You help me have a balanced view of myself and deliver me from any narcissistic ways of thinking or behaving. I ask for open eyes to see and open ears to hear the truth of what You say about me. I know it is okay to love myself, but I pray that the obsession of self is broken off me right now in Jesus name. I command every hindering spirit to go in Jesus name and I ask for help in the renewal of my mind. Convict me, Lord and help me get my face in the Word of God on a consistent and regular basis. In Jesus name, amen.

Pride goes before destruction, and a haughty spirit before a fall. Proverbs 16:18 MEV

Negative

Jesus, You broke the power of sin off my life when You completed Your eternal work on the cross and I accepted You as Savior. Negative thinking, speaking and living is now my choice and I do not have to be controlled by it. Help me to have a better outlook on life. Open my eyes, Lord to all the incredible blessings I have to be thankful for. I have breath in my lungs today and that alone is enough to praise You! I rebuke oppression and command it to go in Jesus name. I loose the outlook of God over my life. In Jesus name, amen.

Finally, brothers, whatever things are true, whatever things are honest, whatever things are just, whatever things are pure, whatever things are lovely, whatever things are of good report, if there is any virtue, and if there is any praise, think on these things. Philippians 4:8 MEV

Nosy

Holy Spirit, help me to mind my own business! I do not have to know every little thing about everybody. Help me to focus on me, my life and my family and leave everything else in Your hands. I praise You, Lord, for You alone are worthy of all my time and attention. In Jesus name, amen.

He who passes by and meddles with strife not belonging to him is like one who takes a dog by the ears. Proverbs 26:17 MEV

Numb

Holy Spirit, come now and invade this space. Invade my heart, mind and soul. I rebuke numbness and command it to go from me right now in Jesus name. Holy Spirit help me to feel again! Bring me back to life. Open my eyes to see Your glorious light. Bring feeling back into my physical body and bring feeling back into my emotions. Help me to love again. Wake me up from this deep sleep! In Jesus name, amen.

It is of the Lord's mercies that we are not consumed; His compassions do not fail. They are new every morning; great is Your faithfulness. "The Lord is my portion," says my soul, "therefore I will hope in Him."Lamentations 3:22-24 MEV

Obedient

Father, help me obey right away! Jesus, You said if I love You I will obey Your commands and Lord, I love You. I repent of ignorance and for living below the standard You have called me to. Reptance does not mean to say I'm sorry, it means to turn from sin and to stop sinning. I choose to repent and be obedient today. If You ask something of me and I do not do it, for me that is sin. Help me to be sensitive to what You're asking of me and help to be led by Your truth, Lord. I praise You for showing me this truth today. In Jesus name, amen.

If you love Me, keep My commandments. John 14:15 MEV

Obsessed

Holy Spirit, You created me to care, but You did not create me to be obsessed with matters outside my control. I lay down my need to control right now in Jesus name. I lay down my need to oversee every tiny little detail and I repent of getting in Your way Lord. Have Your way God, move in the way You see fit. I commit this situation into Your hands and I ask that You move mountains I can't even see to move. I ask that You would work all this out for my good and bring about Your perfect will. Fill me with peace and help me let go. In Jesus name, amen.

"Father, if You are willing, remove this cup from Me. Nevertheless not My will, but Yours, be done." Luke 22:42 MEV

Offended

Father, forgive me for walking into the bait of satan. I repent of offense and I say that today I will forgive. Teach me what it means to truly forgive and help me walk in the ways You have called me to. I release _____ from the prison of my offense. I forgive them, so that I may be forgiven. I did not like what they did to me, Lord. It truly hurt me, but I open the door for You to mend that wound and bring healing to every area of my life. In Jesus name, amen.

For if you forgive men for their sins, your heavenly Father will also forgive you. Matthew 6:14 MEV

Oil

Holy Spirit, I ask for the healing oil of heaven to flow over my body. I pray for a fresh anointing and new boldness to come upon me. The oil of heaven is my portion. You anoint my head with oil and my cup runneth over. I receive what Heaven has for me right now. New ideas, fresh perspective and unfound abilities are coming forth right now. In Jesus name, amen.

You prepare a table before me in the presence of my enemies; You anoint my head with oil; my cup runs over. Psalm 23:5 MEV

Opinions

Father, You did not create me to live by the opinions of man, though You have called me to live in peace with all people. I am not controlled by the opinions of others any longer. I break that hold right now in Jesus name and if through this I have opened a demonic door, I shut it! I command every demonic spirit to go right now in Jesus name. You have no authority or dominion over me. I am a child of God. I am a daughter of the Most High King. I am the head and not the tail. I am above and not below. I will not bow to the opinions of others, but I will, at all times, seek correction and guidance from Holy Spirit. In Jesus name, amen.

For am I now seeking the approval of men or of God? Or am I trying to please men? For if I were still trying to please men, I would not be the servant of Christ. Galatians 1:10 MEV

Organize

Holy Spirit, please help me organize my life in a way that glorifies You. I need help with my organizational skills and I ask to receive the gift of administration right now in Jesus name. I may not come from a super organized background, but that does not mean I cannot create that in my life now through the power of the Holy Spirit. Give me divine ideas and plans to organize my life, home, work place, etc. Surround me with people who can lovingly help me. In Jesus name, amen.

And whatever you do, do it heartily, as for the Lord and not for men, Colossians 3:23 MEV

Over It
Father, I am not afraid to be real with You, because I know You are not afraid to be real with me. I am over it. I am so over it. I need Your help to get through this season. I need Your assistance to love and overcome. Help me Lord. Take me by the hand and rewire my thinking. Give me back my passion and inspire me in a new way. Help me to see this the way You see it. Above all else, I pray that Your will be done on earth as it is in heaven. In Jesus name, amen.

And let us not grow weary in doing good, for in due season we shall reap, if we do not give up. Galatians 6:9 MEV

Panic
Holy Spirit, a fruit of You is peace. I rebuke panic and I command it to go. I take every thought captive and bring it into obedience to the knowledge of Christ. I will not be ran by my emotions or sudden fear. I command fear to go right now in Jesus name. I was given a spirit of love, power and a sound mind. I ask that all of heaven hear my cry. Help me, Lord. Take this from me now in Jesus name. I am free! I am free! I am free! In Jesus name, amen.

Do not be afraid of sudden terror, nor of trouble from the wicked when it comes; for the Lord will be your confidence, and will keep your foot from being caught. Proverbs 3:25-26 MEV

Passion

Father, renew my passion for life. Renew my passion for my marriage, my children and my work place. Help me not be complacent in the arena of life and help me not count the days by. I pray that passion would be ignited in me. Passion that advances Your Kingdom and brings solutions to the problems the world is facing. Put within me creative ideas and birth a new song in me, Lord. I praise You God, because I know You are so excited to answer this prayer. In Jesus name, amen.

He has put a new song in my mouth, even praise to our God; many will see it, and fear, and will trust in the Lord. Psalm 40:3 MEV

Passive Aggressive

Holy Spirit, The Word says that when the apostles asked for boldness You baptized them again in Your Holy Spirit. I ask for boldness to address this heart issue. I repent of being passive aggressive and if I am honest with You and myself; I am sorry for being mean. Help me to fully repent of this, for I know that I cannot do this without the power of Holy Spirit. I pray for deep conviction when my actions do not line up with Your perfect will for my life. I release the song of heaven over my life right now. In Jesus name, amen.

When they had prayed, the place where they were assembled together was shaken. And they were all filled with the Holy

Spirit and spoke the word of God with boldness. Acts 4:31 MEV

Petty

Oh Father, how silly are the ways of the world. What started as a small choice has become a full blown way of life. Open my eyes and remove the scales to how my ignorance has hurt me and others. Heal the broken places and mend these wounds, Lord. Help me to leave behind this mindset of being petty. I ask for a renewed mind in Jesus name. Help me to be consistent and diligent with reading Your word Father. In Jesus name, amen.

Do not be conformed to this world, but be transformed by the renewing of your mind, that you may prove what is the good and acceptable and perfect will of God. Romans 12:2 MEV

Powerful

Oh Lord, You are a God of power. You are unphased by the woes of the world and the intimidation of the enemy. You created me in Your image and You have given me a beautiful gift that I may receive whenever I ask. I ask now to receive the baptism of the Holy Spirit. All of me wants all of You. The Word says that I will receive power when the Holy Spirit has come upon me and I am well aware that advancing Your kingdom on this earth will take power! I receive it now in Jesus name. Surround me with people who will cultivate this in my life. In Jesus name, amen.

Suddenly a sound like a mighty rushing wind came from heaven, and it filled the whole house where they were sitting. There appeared to them tongues as of fire, being distributed and resting on each of them, and they were all filled with the

Holy Spirit and began to speak in other tongues, as the Spirit enabled them to speak. Acts 2:2-4 MEV

Poverty

Father, You are a good God, not one who needs to harm His children to prove a point. You did not create me to live in poverty or lack the daily necessities of life. I rebuke the spirit of poverty and every generational spirit that came along with it right now in Jesus name. Poverty you have no authority or dominion over me and while I won't serve money, I certainly will not serve you either! I will serve Christ alone. Jesus, Your word says that You have given me the power to get wealth. I receive that power now in Jesus name. I loose the spirit of God to move in every area of my life. In Jesus name, amen.

But you must remember the Lord your God, for it is He who gives you the ability to get wealth, so that He may establish His covenant which He swore to your fathers, as it is today. Deuteronomy 8:18 MEV

Prepare

Holy Spirit, prepare me for this next season, prepare me for what is happening and what is going to happen. Prepare me, Lord. Prepare my mind, my heart, my will and my emotions. Show me in Your word how You want to move in my life and I will obey You, Lord. Give me peace and help me quickly discern how You're moving. In Jesus name, amen.

By faith Noah, being warned by God concerning events as yet unseen, in reverent fear constructed an ark for the saving of his household. By this he condemned the world and became an heir of the righteousness that comes by faith. Hebrew 11:7 MEV

Pure

Holy Spirit, put within me a clean and pure heart. Purify my motives and cleanse me from all iniquities. I desire to be a pure expression of Your love on this earth, Lord and I know that I must be pure in heart to do so. I love You, Lord and I want Your perfect will to be done in my life and in the lives of those around me. Use me, God. Use me to show the people You've entrusted to my care just how wonderful You are. In Jesus name, amen.

Create in me a clean heart, O God, and renew a right spirit within me. Psalm 51:10 MEV

Purpose

Father, You created me with a purpose. You created me for good works and I am ready to know exactly what those are. I pray that over the next several days that You would show me what my purpose is. Holy Spirit, I want to know what You are doing on this earth so that I may partner with You. I love You, Lord and above all I want Your perfect will to be done. Show me how I can help that to be done, Lord. In Jesus name, amen.

"Before I formed you in the womb I knew you; and before you were born I sanctified you, and I ordained you a prophet to the nations." Jeremiah 1:5 MEV

Quiet

Father, help me to be quiet and listen, not just speak. Help me to hear Your voice and know exactly what You're saying to me. Help me to realize that prayer is not just a one way conversation, but a beautiful dialogue between You and I. Help me shut out the cares of the world and the woes of this life to fully focus on You. In Jesus name, amen.

Be still and know that I am God; I will be exalted among the nations, I will be exalted in the earth. Psalm 46:10 MEV

Quenched

Oh Holy Spirit, if I have quenched You or grieved You, I repent! Show me how I have done this and help me to quickly make this right. I love You, Holy Spirit and I desire to have Your manifest Presence every moment of every day. Open my eyes to actions, relationships and thought patterns that do not serve You, Lord. In Jesus name, amen.

Do not quench the Spirit. Do not despise prophecies. Examine all things. Firmly hold onto what is good. 1 Thessalonians 5:19-21 MEV

Quit

Father, I am not afraid to be real with You, because I know You are not afraid to be real with me. I want to quit. I want to give up. This seems too hard and I am just so unsure of what I am doing. Please help me, Lord. Holy Spirit, come now and wrap me up in Your arms. Show me Your perfect will for my life. If You want me to stay, I will stay. If You want me to go, I will go. Help me make sound biblical decisions and give me peace that surpasses understanding. In Jesus name, amen.

And let us not grow weary in doing good, for in due season we shall reap, if we do not give up. Galatians 6:9 MEV

Radical

Jesus, Your love for me is radical. You were willing to be beaten, hung naked on a cross and take on death just to build a bridge for me. Knowing that I very well may deny You, You did all this for me, because You knew that if I said yes to Your love; it would all be worth it. My God what a radical love that is. Make me radical like You, Lord. Help me to be bold and totally unashamed like you. Help me to follow You at all cost regardless of what anyone says or thinks. If You loved me that much, I want to love You just the same. In Jesus name, amen.

Neither do men light a candle and put it under a basket, but on a candlestick. And it gives light to all who are in the house. Let your light so shine before men that they may see your good works and glorify your Father who is in heaven. Matthew 5:15-16 MEV

Realistic

Lord, You are not a realistic God and what I consider impossible; You say is possible! Help me not to look at things with a "realistic" lense, but rather a lense of unwavering faith. I walk by faith not by sight. My goals, dreams, visions, and ideas do not have to be realistic to myself or to others, because I know that You are working all things out. I submit all of this to You Lord. In Jesus name, amen.

For with God nothing will be impossible." Luke 1:37 MEV

Religion

Jesus, You did not come to establish a religion, You came to establish a relationship. You walked this earth and gave everything just to know me. I rebuke the spirit of religion and I declare that I will NOT serve religion. It is a vile spirit that only seeks control. I will serve You, Jesus. I will serve Your perfect and Holy will in my life. Deliver me from people, places and things that are controlled by religion and open my eyes to what true relationship with You looks like Jesus. In Jesus name, amen.

You search the Scriptures, because you think in them you have eternal life. These are they who bear witness of Me. John 5:39 MEV

Real

Father, help me to be real with You, myself, and others. Help me to be vulnerable and honest about my feelings, thoughts, and ideas. Help me discern who I should be real with and who I should just be acquaintances with. Help me to understand that I do not have to be "real" with everyone, but I must be real with the people You have divinely placed in my life. Break off trust issues and false mindsets that tell me I need to put on a mask to be loved. In Jesus name, amen.

Trust in Him at all times; you people, pour out your heart before Him; God is a shelter for us. Selah Psalms 62:8 MEV

Relax

Jesus, I know that You know stress. I know You know what it is like to feel stress far beyond what the physical body can handle. Help me to relax, Lord. Help me take a deep breath and just relax. I rebuke guilt and shame for simply taking care of myself. Help me obey and enjoy the Sabbath that You graciously established for me. Open doors for me to truly relax, Lord. Give me more meaningful time with my family and give me great favor in the workplace. In Jesus name, amen.

Then He said to them, "The Sabbath was made for man, and not man for the Sabbath. Mark 2:27 MEV

Rest

Jesus, You said that You would carry the heavy burden of life and I would only need to be led by Your yoke. I receive now deep rest for my spirit and soul. Show me what this looks like in my life. Heal every broken place in my life that comes from a lack of rest and give me a new understanding of how important rest is. Help me not to overwork for I know that my efforts are in vain if they are not led by You. Thank You Lord. I know You're so excited to answer this prayer. In Jesus name, amen.

On the seventh day God completed His work which He had done, and He rested on the seventh day from all His work which He had done. Then God blessed the seventh day and made it holy, because on it He had rested from all His work which He had created and made. Genesis 2:2-3 MEV

Resent
Holy Spirit, I open the door for You to come in and heal every resentful place in my life. Every area of my life that I know about and even the areas I don't know about. I repent of holding on to this for so long and I ask now that this be completely taken from my life.

Heal me, O Lord, and I will be healed; save me, and I will be saved, for You are my praise. Jeremiah 17:14 MEV

Salvation
Jesus, I believe You are the savior. I believe that You walked this earth as truly God and man. I believe You were born of a virgin and that You lived without sin. I believe You died on the cross to pay the penalty for sin. I believe You rose three days later and conquered death forever. I ask You to be the Lord of my life, Jesus. I invite You to fill every place in my life. I give You my life fully. I ask for forgiveness for my sins. I repent and ask for the help of the Holy Spirit to walk this out on a daily basis. Help me, Lord. I am not perfect, but I want You, forever. In Jesus name, amen.

that if you confess with your mouth Jesus is Lord, and believe in your heart that God has raised Him from the dead, you will be saved Romans 10:9 MEV

If you prayed this prayer and believed it with all your heart, the Bible says that you have been born again. I highly encourage you to connect with a group of fellow Christians and a local church. See prayer Powerful and take the next steps in your Christian faith (baptism of the Holy Spirit and water baptism). Begin reading the Bible, now! Today! Download the free ESV Bible App and begin in the book of Matthew (it's my favorite book).

Secret
Father, I know that I cannot keep a secret from You for You are all knowing, but if I am telling the truth; I still try. I repent of letting my secrets and my deep concerns keep me out of Your Presence. Help me be totally open and honest with You, Lord. Cleanse me from the secrets of my life and help me make decisions You're calling me to. In Jesus name, amen.

or there is nothing covered that will not be revealed, or hidden that will not be known. Therefore what you have said in the darkness will be heard in the light. And what you have whispered in the ear in private rooms will be proclaimed on the housetops. 12:2-3 MEV

Selfish
Jesus, You gave it all for me. You were the most selfless person to walk this earth and You have called me to walk in Your ways. I repent of being so self centered. Deliver me from this mindset and help me to walk this out. Holy Spirit I invite You to invade every area of my life, including the area of self

will and self interest. Help me have a balanced view of myself and others. In Jesus name, amen.

Let nothing be done out of strife or conceit, but in humility let each esteem the other better than himself. Philipians 2:3 MEV

Sex
Prayer of repentance
Father, You created sex to be between a man and a woman in the context of marriage. Heal me from the wound of my sin. I break every ungodly soul tie and I call back my soul right now in Jesus name. I pray for forgiveness for any sexual sin I committed before marriage. I command every demonic spirit that came in through sex to go right now in Jesus name. I ask for complete healing in my mind, will, emotions and physical body. I repent, Lord! Help me turn from this sin once and for all. Cleanse me of all ungodliness and put within me a clean heart with an unshakable desire for holiness. In Jesus name, amen.

Escape from sexual immorality. Every sin that a man commits is outside the body. But he who commits sexual immorality sins against his own body. 1 Corinthians 6:18 MEV

Therefore this is what the LORD says: "If you repent, I will restore you that you may serve me; if you utter worthy, not worthless, words, you will be my spokesman. Let this people turn to you, but you must not turn to them. Jeremiah 15:19 NIV

Prayer for married couples
Father, You created sex to be between a man and a woman in the context of marriage. You are not afraid of sex nor do You shun or overlook it. In fact, You celebrate it! I pray for deep sexual passion in my marriage. Give my husband eyes for me

alone and give me eyes for him only. I pray for a spark that never burns out. Help me to please my husband and help him to please me. Thank you for this beautiful union, Lord. In Jesus name, amen.

Do not deprive one another, except perhaps by agreement for a limited time, that you may devote yourselves to prayer; but then come together again, so that Satan may not tempt you because of your lack of self-control. 1 Corinthians 7:9-10 MEV

Skeptical
Holy Spirit, deliver me from distrust. I rebuke the spirit of fear and I loose love, power, and a sound mind. I do not have to be skeptical of everyone and everything. Lord, forgive me for how this has hindered meaningful relationships in my life. Heal any trust issues I have in my heart. Holy Spirit, I invite you to begin to peel back the layers of this wound and heal me from the inside out. In Jesus name, amen.

You will seek me and find me when you seek me with all your heart. Jeremiah 29:13 NIV

Shy
Holy Spirit, make me bold! Help to have conversations that stretch me and get me out of my comfort zone. Help me be brave to go and do the things I truly desire to. I rebuke a spirit of fear and anxiety. I was given love, power and a sound mind. I will walk in that. Help me create friendships, atmospheres and environments that I love and feel free to be myself in. In Jesus name, amen.

Now, Lord, look on their threats and grant that Your servants may speak Your word with great boldness, Acts 4:39 MEV

Spirit

Jesus, You are spirit and truth. No one can come to the Father except through You. I surrender fully to being led by Your spirit. Your Holy Spirit that was poured out on the earth by You. Introduce me to Holy Spirit and help me get to know Him. Holy Spirit, I want a real relationship with You. I want to know what You love and what grieves You. I want to feel Your Presence every minute of every day. In Jesus name, amen.

When the day of Pentecost had come, they were all together in one place. Suddenly a sound like a mighty rushing wind came from heaven, and it filled the whole house where they were sitting. There appeared to them tongues as of fire, being distributed and resting on each of them, and they were all filled with the Holy Spirit and began to speak in other tongues, as the Spirit enabled them to speak. Acts 2:2-4 MEV

Success

Father, thank You for giving me the power to get wealth. (Deuteronomy 8:18) I pray that You would bless everything my hand touches. I pray that You prosper me in all my ways. I pray that my success would glorify You and I commit all my success to You even now. Breathe on my efforts, Lord. Breathe on my business, my work place, my ministry, my home, my marriage, my investments, and everything concerning me. I know that Your promises are yes and amen! I believe and I walk in the reality that I am a child of God. Thank You, Lord! In Jesus name, amen.

So they rose up early in the morning and went out to the Wilderness of Tekoa. And when they went out, Jehoshaphat stood and said, "Listen to me, Judah and those dwelling in Jerusalem. Believe in the Lord your God, and you will be supported. Believe His prophets, and you will succeed." 2 Chronicles 20:20 MEV

Tears

Father, You have caught every tear. You do not miss a single thing that is going on in my life, Lord. I pray that You would wipe these tears and help me through this situation. You know it, Lord. You know it even more that I do. I invite Holy Spirit in this and I receive peace that surpasses understanding. In Jesus name, amen.

You have kept count of my tossings; put my tears in your bottle. Are they not in your book? Psalm 56:8 MEV

Testimony

Revelation 12:11 tells me that I will overcome the enemy by the blood of the lamb and the word of my testimony. Holy Spirit, make me bold! Help me to tell what You have done in my life, so that others may be set free too. I commit my mouth into Your hands, Lord. Use me! Use my life! Use my salvation story! May thousands more come to know You through my story. Breathe on this. In Jesus name, amen.

And they have conquered him by the blood of the Lamb and by the word of their testimony, for they loved not their lives even unto death. Revelation 12:11 MEV

Tithe

Father, You set the tithe. You ask 10% of every dollar that comes into my house. I thank You Lord for putting this system in place so Your Kingdom can be advanced on this earth. I pray that You would help me be obedient to not only give my tithe, but do so with a cheerful heart. I pray over the tithes of my church and I ask You to multiply them. Help the leaders of

my church advance Your Kingdom and be sensitive to You,
Holy Spirit. In Jesus name, amen.

*Bring the full tithe into the storehouse, that there may be food
in my house. And thereby put me to the test, says the Lord of
hosts, if I will not open the windows of heaven for you and
pour down for you a blessing until there is no more need. I will
rebuke the devourer[a] for you, so that it will not destroy the
fruits of your soil, and your vine in the field shall not fail to
bear, says the Lord of hosts. Then all nations will call you
blessed, for you will be a land of delight, says the Lord of
hosts. Malachi 3:10-12 MEV*

Tolerant
Jesus, You loved all, but You never tolerated sin. You dealt
with those who claimed to know You, but lived in blatant sin
differently than those who didn't know You at all. I pray that
You would help me understand this revelation and study it out
for myself. Help me to not tolerate the things that are not of
You. Instead, help me to be a light for those lost in darkness.
Make me bold, Lord. In Jesus name, amen.

Tradition
Holy Spirit, reveal it to me if I have traded the truth of Your
word for the traditions of man. I repent of following any
tradition that does not align with Your word. Lord, I don't
desire the tradition of my church or family or anything else for
that matter, more than I want the truth of You. I desire to
please You and advance Your Kingdom on this earth. Give me
ears to hear and eyes to see, Lord. In Jesus name, amen.

*in vain do they worship me, teaching as doctrines the
commandments of men. You leave the commandment of God
and hold to the tradition of men." And he said to them, "You*

have a fine way of rejecting the commandment of God in order to establish your tradition! Mark 7:7-9 MEV

Ugly
Father, I have been made in the image of You. I am beautiful, because I am created by You. I pray that You help me to see just how much You love me and from that place I hope to love myself. I rebuke the lies of the enemy right now in Jesus name. If there are people in my life who speak against the God given identity that You desire for me, cause them to repent or remove them from my life. In Jesus name, amen.

He has made everything beautiful in its time. Also, he has put eternity into man's heart, yet so that he cannot find out what God has done from the beginning to the end. Ecclesiastes 3:11 MEV

Uncertain
Lord, I ask for the wisdom of heaven right now in Jesus name. I pray that You would give me clarity and peace about the decision You want me to make. Lead me with Your peace, Lord. I thank You for caring about every situation in my life. In Jesus name, amen.

If any of you lacks wisdom, let him ask God, who gives generously to all without reproach, and it will be given him. James 1:5 MEV

Useless
Jesus, You did not die for junk! You died for me, because You loved me just as I was; just as I am. I was created for a purpose. I have good works that You have set for me to do. Show me what those are, Lord. Direct me, Holy Spirit. Show me what You are doing, Holy Spirit and open my eyes to how I

can partner with You right now. I am more than useful in the Kingdom of God. In Jesus name, amen.

For we are his workmanship, created in Christ Jesus for good works, which God prepared beforehand, that we should walk in them. Ephesians 2:10 MEV

Virgin

Father, I praise You for preserving my purity. I thank You, Holy Spirit for helping me to overcome temptation and save myself for the man You desire to be my husband. You have kept me as a pure and spotless bride through the washing of Your word. I pray You help me for I know this is a holy and beautiful thing. I commit myself to You, Holy Spirit. In Jesus name, amen.

But if they cannot exercise self-control, they should marry. For it is better to marry than to burn with passion. 1 Corinthians 7:9 MEV

Vulgar

Father, You created all of me to glorify You. I repent of vulgar and seductive behaviors. I rebuke and bind the spirit of jezebel and I command it to go right now in Jesus name. I loose truth and the glory of God over my life. Lord, remove anyone in my life who is an open door to this spirit. Help me walk in holiness all the days of my life. I love You, Lord. I will serve Jesus Christ and Him alone. In Jesus name, amen.

To deliver you from the strange woman, From the adulteress who flatters with her words; That leaves the companion of her youth And forgets the covenant of her God; For her house sinks down to death And her tracks lead to the dead Proverbs 2:16-19 MEV

Vulnerable

Father, help me to be vulnerable; especially with my husband. Help me to open up and allow others in. Heal the places of my heart that hold me back. Help me laugh more freely, cry when I need to, and look others in the eyes intently. Help me to share my thoughts and feelings. Help me connect with others, but most of all; help me connect with You. In Jesus name, amen.

"But he said to me, "My grace is sufficient for you, for my power is made perfect in weakness." Therefore I will boast all the more gladly of my weaknesses, so that the power of Christ may rest upon me. For the sake of Christ, then, I am content with weaknesses, insults, hardships, persecutions, and calamities. For when I am weak, then I am strong."
Corinthians 12:9-10 MEV

Weak

Holy Spirit, when I am weak, You are strong! Show me what this means in my daily life. I invite You to invade this situation. I pray that I would be strengthened through this revelation. In Jesus name, amen.

"But he said to me, "My grace is sufficient for you, for my power is made perfect in weakness." Therefore I will boast all the more gladly of my weaknesses, so that the power of Christ may rest upon me. For the sake of Christ, then, I am content with weaknesses, insults, hardships, persecutions, and calamities. For when I am weak, then I am strong."
Corinthians 12:9-10 MEV

Worth

Jesus, You said I was worth dying for. You determined my worth by the price You were willing to pay to have me. You held nothing back. You left Your throne in heaven and died an earthly death just to build a bridge for me. You decided I was worthy of relationship with You, because You died for me. Help me to realize that I am worth much more than my earthly eyes can see. Help me to deeply study my identity as a Christian, so I may know just who You say I am. In Jesus name, amen.

Worry
Father, I ask for peace that surpasses understanding. I rebuke fear and anxiety. I command it to go right now in Jesus name. I surrender all of this to You, Jesus. I see myself laying this at Your feet right now. I will not pick this back up. Your burden is easy and Your yoke is light. I receive total peace right now. In Jesus name, amen.

Proverbs 12:25 Anxiety in a man's heart weighs him down, but a good word makes him glad.
Cast all your anxiety on him because he cares for you. 1 Peter 5:7
Do not be anxious about anything, but in everything by prayer and supplication with thanksgiving let your requests be made known to God. Philippians 4:6-7 MEV

Why
Father, I don't understand, but I trust You. In Jesus name, amen.

And he said, "Naked I came from my mother's womb, and naked shall I return. The Lord gave, and the Lord has taken away; blessed be the name of the Lord." Job 1:21 MEV

Yell

Holy Spirit, take over my life. I ask to receive the gift of tongues right now in Jesus name. Help me, Lord. I do not want to be driven by anger and emotion a moment longer. I want to be the woman, wife, mother and daughter You have called me to be. Please heal the relationships I have damaged. I release the power of God into my life and situation right now. In Jesus name, amen.

Even a fool who keeps silent is considered wise; when he closes his lips, he is deemed intelligent. Proverbs 17:28 MEV

Yourself

Father, I know that I cannot love anyone else more than I love myself. I realize that the more I try to love others while neglecting myself the more I perpetuate this cycle. Help me to take a breath and take care of myself. I pray that You would help me and lead me. Show me what it means to love myself, Lord. I pray that above everything else that my life glorifies You. In Jesus name, amen.

The second is this: 'You shall love your neighbor as yourself.' There is no other commandment greater than these." Mark 12:31 MEV

Zeal

Holy Spirit, I want to please You! I want to be on fire for You and I want that fire to be seen by all those who walk into my life. Put a zeal that cannot be shaken within me. A zeal to serve You, lead others to You and zeal for the wisdom of Your word. In Jesus name, amen.

Do not be slothful in zeal, be fervent in spirit, serve the Lord. Romans 12:11 MEV

Unless otherwise stated all scriptures used are from the English Standard Version.